FLY FOR YOU

J. ANTON DAVIS

All Points Creative, LLC

Copyright © 2024 J. Anton Davis

All rights reserved. No portion of this book may be reproduced, stored in a retrieval system, or transmitted in any form or by any means – electronic, mechanical, photocopy, recording, scanning, or other – except for brief quotations in critical reviews or articles, without the prior written permission of the publisher.

Published by All Points Creative, LLC.

Many of the poems in this collection were previously published by J. Anton Davis on his Substack, @jantonpoetry, or his website, JAntonPoetry.com, and subsequently shared on various social media platforms.

Cover © 2024 by J. Anton Davis

Website: JAntonPoetry.com
Substack: @jantonpoetry
Instagram: @jantonpoetry
X: @jantonpoetry
Facebook: J. Anton Poetry
Goodreads: J. Anton Davis

All Points Creative, LLC
P.O. Box 98232
Raleigh, North Carolina 27624

978-1-7355407-7-1 (Paperback)
978-1-7355407-8-8 (eBook)

DEDICATION

To my incredible wife, Alexandra,
and my sweet boys, James and Liam.
I will always do my best
to fly for you.

CONTENTS

Dreams 1

Fly For You 2

As I Sit Here 3

The Edge of the World 4

In My Dreams… 5

Simple Dreams 6

Faulty Scales 7

To Know 8

Watering Flowers 10

Simple Creatures 11

Beyond the Horizon 13

Unseen Efforts 14

Creators and Critics 17

The Life of an Artist 18

Sowing and Reaping 20

Artists and Critics	21
…Can He Even Paint?	23
Birds on a Line	24
Will You Stop Me?	25
Admiration	27
I Knew	28
Chasing Shadows	30
Those We Love	33
I Still Remember	34
Baby Boy	35
Sturdy Roots	36
Hold Him Now	38
Irresistible Magic	40
Little One	42
Free Time for Parents	43
A Fond Memory	44
Halcyon Romance	46

The Gift is Mine	47
Community	49
Contagion	50
Satisfaction	52
You Loved Me Well	53
Thanksgiving Plus-One	55
Sentimental	57
Tightly Bound	59
Existence	61
Fireflies	62
The Sun Still Burns	64
I Am Here	66
What Shall I Do With the Wall?	67
A Bell Rings	69
The Growth of Flowers	70
The Line	71
Predictable Distance	73

Innocent Beauty	74
I'm Asking You	75
Falling Skies	76
Grief	77
Do You Hear Me?	79
Desert Flowers?	80
Change	81
Do You Hear the Rooster Crowing?	82
As We Wait for Fall	83
An Adult's Lament	84
Old Stones	86
The Last Leaf of Autumn	88
Perspective	91
Insects in Lamplight	92
And So It Goes	94
Cursing the Sun	95
Beautiful Brokenness	97

Connection	98
With Grace	99
Noble or Reckless?	101
The Green Thumb Delusion	102
Cursing Trees	103
The Rose Has Thorns	104
Wisdom	105
One Year	106
Like Son Like Father	108
A Line in the Sand	110
Someone I Once Knew	112
You Said You Wanted	113
A Desperate Ear	115
When a Dog Bites	116
Mountaintop	117
Self-Confidence	120
Broad Searches	121

Insanity	122
I Sold My Guitar	123
Voiceless	124
I Paid it Twice	125
Beware the Knocking at Your Door	126
Knowledge	128
Lament	**129**
Discontentment	130
Heartless	132
We Used to Walk the Path Together	133
Esse Quam Videri	135
This World	136
In My Haste	139
Prophets	140
The Buried Lead	141
A Thousand Pearled Oysters	142
Overkill	144

Human Nature	145
Of Puppies and Rabbits	147
Consider	149
Seaworthy Ships	150
Puddle Jumping	152
The Last to Drink	153
Tug of War	155
When Glass Breaks	156
The Death of "Me"	157
Take Heart	159
A Ray of Sunlight	160
Rejection	161
Simple Certainties	162
Finding Freedom	163
Facing Lions	165
A Light Among Death	170
Audacious Life	172

The Beach Reeds Sway	174
Unseen Efforts	176
Me	179
"Other"	180
I Am Who I Am	182
Peacemaker	183
You Liked My Smile	184
Wind-Up Doll	185
Like Me	187
I'm No Fun	189
Wanderer	190
Remembering	191
Treehouse	192
Free	194
Me. I Do.	195
Summer Days	198
A Softer Kiss	199

Avoiding Sleep 200

FLY FOR YOU

J. ANTON DAVIS

PROLOGUE

Regardless of your current age, you likely fall into one of three categories:

> 1. You have yet to haul a box of old school notes, binders, and books – some of which are 5, 10, or 20+ years old – from apartment to apartment or house to house.
>
> 2. You currently have in your custody the box referenced in Category 1.
>
> 3. You once had in your custody the box referenced in Category 1 and decided at some point that enough was enough and it had to go!

Finally, at 37 years old, I got rid of my last-remaining high school, college, and law school notebooks. While there is no legitimate excuse for how long that process took me to complete, there is one culprit that unquestioningly added to the delay; poetry. Beginning in middle school, I started writing poems here and there in my school notebooks when my mind would wander in class. Due to this practice, I have never gotten rid of an old spiralbound notebook without first flipping quickly through each page, just in case there may be a poem or two hidden inside. Is this practice because these old poems have any shred of redeeming, literary qualities? I answer that question with a sincere, emphatic, "*NO!*" I continue this practice because I love being reminded that poetry has always been an important part of my life and self-expression. Maybe one day those lost-and-found poems will see the light of day, but only when my reputation hits such a low point that even those terrible poems couldn't damage it any further.

Today, as in those earlier days of my life, poetry

helps me to dream, mourn, celebrate, and think. It is something about the way my mind – and the minds of countless others – works, that there are certain feelings or thoughts I am not sure I could express or make sense of in any other way. Some people paint, others do woodwork, and still others play video games. We all do something to help our minds process, rest, stretch, and grow. For me, especially when wrestling with powerful emotions or heady concepts, poetry allows me to exist within a world where my words can at least come vaguely close to expressing the immensity of a crushing loss, a great accomplishment, or a jawdropping truth. In poetry there are no limits, so processing through poetry allows me to wrestle with feelings and concepts that themselves feel limitless.

While poetry plays this vital role in my life, I know that my children will likely find other means through which they come to understand life and the world around them. And that's fine! I want them to live authentically and approach the world in ways that complement their unique wiring. What I can't allow, to the extent that I have any ability to stop it, is for my children to fail to pursue those things that give them life and light a fire in their eyes – unless, of course, they intentionally forgo those desires for something they deem even greater. It is these thoughts that led to the poem, *Fly for you*, from which this book derives its name.

I realized one night that while I can tell my children over and over that they can do anything and that they should follow their dreams, if my children do not see me even attempt to pursue my own dreams they may one day take me at my actions and not my words. They may write off my "you-can-do-anything" encouragement as some sort of naïve, Pollyanna platitude, instead of the sincere, sober words of a father who doesn't want them to limit themselves in any way. If, however, I *show* them what following one's dreams looks like, they will have no choice but to believe me when I say they can do it, too.

Sharing my poetry publicly, while only slightly less intimidating than it was when I first started doing it five or so years ago, is one way I chase my dreams. I hope this book encourages not only my children to fly high, but you as well. Thank you for reading and I hope you enjoy this collection of poems!

FLY FOR YOU

J. ANTON DAVIS

Dreams

J. ANTON DAVIS

FLY FOR YOU

If I only tell you,
"You can fly,"
you may believe me
or you may not,
but if I fly,
you'll know it's true,
so I'll do my best
to fly for you.

AS I SIT HERE

As I sit here, filling time,
the bells atop Saint Peter's chime,
the gawkers at the Duomo climb,
as I sit here filling time.

As I sit here, mouse in hand,
a tourist walks Moroccan sand,
a southern Spanish brow is fanned,
as I sit here, mouse in hand.

As I sit here, lit by screens,
a trav'ler crosses English greens,
a tour guide talks of kings and queens,
as I sit here, lit by screens.

For future joys I now prepare,
for when I leave behind my chair,
to taste the fresh, unspoiled air,
for future joys I now prepare.

J. ANTON DAVIS

THE EDGE OF THE WORLD

Have you ever been
to the edge of the world,
where everything inside you
screams to go back,
warning that you have ventured too far,
but something pushes you
forward, past the walls
of fear and self-doubt,
past the well-worn path
that would guide your retreat
into the truly unknown,
where not even the smell
of something familiar
lingers in the air?

I have once been
to the edge of the world,
and it freed my soul.

IN MY DREAMS…

Though bound we are
by place, it seems,
I've crossed the cosmos
in my dreams...

SIMPLE DREAMS

Simple dreams
are the best, it seems.

The mind of a child
is fertile and wild.

The former the root,
the latter the fruit.

FAULTY SCALES

Often
we choose
a lifetime
of regret
instead of a month,
a year, a decade,
of hard work
in the pursuit
of something
we truly desire.

What scales
do we use
where a lifetime
weighs so little,
and a fraction
of time
so much?

TO KNOW

In relation to one's calling,
ignorance is not bliss;
it is confusion
and frustration,
wandering
and wondering,
discontentment
and dissatisfaction.

Better to work every day
as a laborer, knowing
in your heart
that you are a painter,
than to paint every day
and not know why.

The knowing laborer
can dream
while he works,
envisioning the days
when he might paint
from dawn until dusk,

reveling in his thoughts
as if that were his reality.

If the aimless painter
dreams at all,
it is of fickle ventures
and plans that change
as often as the moon
does in its cycle.

Truly,
it is better to know
your calling
and not do it
than to do
your calling
and not know it.

One has clarity and hope,
the other, only confusion
and doubt.

WATERING FLOWERS

Can one sincerely hope to save,
a wilted flower from the grave,
will not the time and effort yield,
the withered still to death a slave?

Or is there hope for one to coax,
the blossom to reveal the hoax,
that feigning death was meant to spur,
the longing that the death evokes?

SIMPLE CREATURES

We are only
simple creatures,
pleased by so much less
than we would guess,
able to endure
so much more
than our fears suggest.

Our lives revolve
around pleasure and pain,
sad truth or not,
it seems it's our lot,
but won't we at least
trade famine for feast
and choose real over rot?

A lone drop of rain
bests a spurious sea
and a counterfeit dream
cannot glisten or gleam,
so go find what is true
that is deep inside you

and let still waters teem.

BEYOND THE HORIZON

It is not a hatred of home
that sends a bird southward,
but an inexplicable yearning
for something
beyond the horizon.

UNSEEN EFFORTS

I walked one step
and no one cared,
then at one hundred
one man stared,

five hundred earned
a clap or two,
one thousand felt
like déjà vu,

three thousand won
a little crowd,
five thousand made
some cheer aloud,

eight thousand brought
the local news,
ten thousand spurred
some interviews,

one hundred thousand
steps I strode,

FLY FOR YOU

before the fame
and fortune flowed,

still millions cried,
"He must be new!"
but I knew
that it wasn't true...

Creators and Critics

THE LIFE OF AN ARTIST

How many artists
have died unknown,
striving, creating,
and dreaming alone,
thanklessly working
themselves to the bone,
how many artists
have died unknown?

How many artists
have died depressed,
wailing and weeping
and beating their chest,
constantly wary
but finding no rest,
how many artists
have died depressed?

How many artists
have lived at ease,
dreaming and doing
their work as they please,

FLY FOR YOU

no deadlines to fear
or boss to appease,
how many artists
have lived at ease?

How many artists
have lived inspired,
joyfully working
no matter how tired,
searching for beauty,
not objects acquired,
how many artists
have lived inspired?

The life of an artist
is often a dance,
between both heartbreak
and stunning romance,
a daring adventure,
a taking of chance,
the life of an artist
is often a dance.

J. ANTON DAVIS

SOWING AND REAPING

Whether you plow the earth
with a brush or a pen,
the way to grow
a successful crop
is not by amassing buyers,
but by faithfully
and methodically
planting seed after seed,
day after day,
month after month.

Whether it is one year
or one hundred
before a single soul
discovers your land,
it will not be littered
with the shreddings
of well-laid plans,
reports, or almanacs,
but magnificent crops
as far as the eye can see.

ARTISTS AND CRITICS

Though artists and critics
can seem
like two sides
of the same coin,
as often
both stand
in close proximity
to one another,
they could not be
more dissimilar.

An artist
needs no other person
to exist;
he needs only
to make art.

A critic
has no inherent existence,
but is a response to
and consequence of
an artist

first creating.

Without the artist,
there can be no critic,
but the critic's absence
hinders neither brush
nor pen.

...CAN HE EVEN PAINT?

I sculpted a masterpiece
second to none,
with textures and colors
that danced in the sun,
the detail was expert,
the polish, divine,
thematically deep
in a simple design,
the art world applauded,
the everyman cheered,
and even my fair-weather fans
reappeared,
though one critic leveled
the oddest complaint,
saying, "Sure, he can sculpt,
but can he even paint?"

...my eyes rolled so hard
that I thought I would faint.

BIRDS ON A LINE

Birds
just sitting
on a line,
shuffling,
rustling,
jockeying
for a place
and a view
of the passersby,
each note sung
as if divine,
though shrill and biting
as a squawk or whine,
each feathery drone
content to sit
and gripe and moan
in comfort, set apart
on a sagging throne,
jesters holding court
on twine...what more
should one expect
of birds on a line?

WILL YOU STOP ME?

Will you stop me,
with all your bluster
and intimidation,
with your weapons
of shame and humiliation
and your words
seeking nothing
but the degradation
of my soul and my heart
and all that I am,
will you stop me,
can you stop me,
when my words rush forth
like the torrents that surge
from a crumbling dam,
overtaking all
with the force and subtlety
of a battering ram,
will you stand against these floods
and hope to remain dry?
Please try.

Admiration

I KNEW

I knew,
I knew
when I started
reading you
I'd find a sage,
weaving wisdom
into every word,
through every page,
flaunting your brilliance
as a lion flaunts its strength,
simply by being.

I knew,
I knew
when I started
reading you
that I would come
to love you
as a sister, charmed
by your strength
and wit, stunned
by your pride

and daring.

I knew,
I knew
when I started
reading you
that I would look
to find you
and discover
how close
you once were,
but are no longer,
my long-lost, literary
grandmother.

CHASING SHADOWS

What would we give
to meet those
who have come before us,
to shake their hands
and ask them their secrets,
to tell them how much
their words have meant
to us, how their courage
to share their gifts,
in their time,
reaches still today
across the ages
to comfort lonely souls
who cannot find anyone living
that speaks their language.

It triggers
almost a feeling
of mourning to know
that some conversations
will never be,
but thank God

that those giants of other eras
shared themselves
with not only the few
who breathed while they did,
but with the many
who never had that pleasure.

With that said,
I am almost certain
that even if I could
step back in time
and converse with my many teachers,
they would be no more extraordinary
than those living today,
except in that most important
of traits among men,
that each chose
to subject themselves
to the barbs and arrows
of their time
in order to share
what had to be shared.

Those We Love

J. ANTON DAVIS

I STILL REMEMBER

I still remember
the din of shoppers
lolling me to sleep
against your shoulder,
the smell of candles,
donuts, and perfume
momentarily piquing my senses
as we passed by
different shops and stands,
my inner world completely calm
as the outer world passed me by
like some sort of pleasant dream,
close enough to experience
but with no power to harm me
or even engage with me;
I was free in your arms, truly resting,
the peace of my mind, heart,
and body attesting
that you were strong,
that you were safe,
that you were good.

BABY BOY

Can I say, "I love you," enough times
that you'll remember when I'm gone
the pride I felt
when I first knelt
and held you in my arms?

Can I kiss your cheeks so often
that you'll always feel my love,
the tears I wept
when you first slept
with our own roof above?

I love you so much, baby boy,
if nothing, let this poem be
a never-ending gift to you
from your old man who somehow grew
to love a child so tenderly.

STURDY ROOTS

I sometimes mourn
a simple thought,
that though
my memories are sweet
with my two sons,
five weeks and one,
the mind of each is incomplete.

Though I remember vividly
the moment when
I met each one,
they won't recall
those days at all
or anything
for years to come.

But I must trust,
as they grow up,
that one day
they will know the fruits
of moments sown
through years unknown,

FLY FOR YOU

their wild, winding,
and sturdy roots.

HOLD HIM NOW

You wish
you'd held him more
when he lay swaddled
in a thin, cotton blanket,
cheeks for days
surrounding babbling lips
and bright eyes;
hold him now.

You wish
you'd built more
sandcastles together
when he first toddled
around the beach,
sunscreen smeared
down his red face,
focused only
on whatever small project
held his fickle attention;
build with him now.

You wish

FLY FOR YOU

you'd played more
games of catch
when he broke in his first mitt,
throwing with the clunky mechanics
of a newly minted ball player,
backyard-trained and wholly untested;
throw with him now.

No matter the moments
you're sure you've missed
or the seasons of life
you're certain you took for granted,
do what you can now, today;
toss that ball,
give that advice,
teach that skill,
or share that trip,
but don't spend
even a moment
lamenting what wasn't,
focusing instead
on what could be
and then making it so.

IRRESISTIBLE MAGIC

We stood together in the water,
waves rhythmically wrapping
against my shins
as you sat still in my arms,
your eyes and mine set to the sea,
father and son breathing deep
the salt air, heavy wind,
and irresistible magic of the ocean.

You didn't want to touch the water,
and I didn't make you;
why shame you for perceiving,
even at your young age,
the immense power of the ocean,
the strength of the waves,
and the unpredictability of the surf?

No, I was happy to hold you,
staring silently together at the chaos
and order of it all, knowing deep down
that the calming, disquieting mass
reflected our own lives,

FLY FOR YOU

where undefined nothings
become clearly defined somethings,
and where razor-sharp edges
dissolve into hazy whisps
of light and color.

LITTLE ONE

What worthy pilferer of sleep
could hope to oust this little one,
my sleep is never better spent
than when I'm comforting my son.

FREE TIME FOR PARENTS

One day I woke to realize
I had free time, to my surprise,
I celebrated with a sigh,
and *poof,* the day had passed me by.

J. ANTON DAVIS

A FOND MEMORY

Tonight, I lived
a fond memory.

I knew
while we sat
in the dimly lit darkness,
rocking forward and backward,
our thoughts as free
as a wandering balloon,
that the moment
I was living
would one day be
a fond memory,
the kind that makes
your chest swell
and your voice catch,
if only for a moment.

You were there,
across the peaceful darkness,
watching a curious cat
prowl a lonely street;

FLY FOR YOU

the cicadas hummed
a sweet southern tune,
the kind that lingers
in your ears
as you fade off to sleep,
reminding you
that everything
will be all right,
that no other problems
must be solved tonight.

Tonight, I lived
a fond memory,
and you were there,
the secret to it all.

HALCYON ROMANCE

We traveled the world,
just me and you,
and no one knew,
no one knew.

THE GIFT IS MINE

Often, I write
after my wife
has gone to bed,
finding it to be
the best time of day
to think
and to process.

Whenever I finish,
I get into bed
and give her
a kiss
on the cheek
or forehead.

I learned recently
that these kisses
almost always
go unnoticed,
as her hummed responses
are never remembered
in the morning.

It struck me,
when considering
this fact,
that her lack of knowledge
takes nothing away
from these moments,
as every time
I kiss her,
the gift is mine.

Community

J. ANTON DAVIS

CONTAGION

What spreads
through communities
like a drop of ink
in water,
needing only
one point of origin
to leap from person
to person until
all are infected?

What moves effortlessly
between people
with only the slightest brush
of contact, a force which,
once detected, has traveled
with such imperceptible speed
that it is impossible
to determine
its original host?

What spurs leaders,

stuns nations,
and consumes man
from the inside out?

Love.

SATISFACTION

Give me a weekend
with family and friends
and I
could die
with a full heart
and quiet mind,
with nothing left
to satisfy.

YOU LOVED ME WELL

You came for me with blade in hand,
you didn't speak,
you didn't yell,
you didn't even bat an eye
when I told you to go to hell,
from left to right, then right to left,
you slashed across my haughty chest,
I held my breath
and braced for pain,
for steal to cut
through skin and vein,
but nothing happened...
had you missed?
Could luck so marvelous
exist?
I looked at you,
then I looked down,
and there lay dying
on the ground
some fetid leech,
some vile mound,
that twitched

then stopped
without a sound.

How did you know,
how did you see
the parasite consuming me?
Though it was latched
upon my chest,
I never knew,
I never guessed,
if not for you
I'd soon have died
by slow and steady
homicide,
forgive me, friend,
you loved me well,
when I told you
to go to hell...

THANKSGIVING PLUS-ONE

The glasses clink,
the turkey dwindles,
the fading fire,
with help, rekindles,
the laughter and the love
abound,
an older man is bathed
and gowned.

The Rockettes dance,
the show dogs trot,
the cider simmers,
piping hot,
the football flies,
the eyelids fall,
a woman longs
to walk the hall.

The puzzles pour,
the game dice roll,
the pages turn,
the fingers scroll,

the must-goes warm,
the coffee pours,
a nurse checks in
on aches and sores.

The room phone rings,
the spirit lifts,
a smile returns,
the posture shifts,
the caller "Hi"s,
the called "Hello"s,
the distance fades,
the guest list grows.

SENTIMENTAL

We are all
a bit sentimental,
aren't we?

The most
meaningless object
could be our most
prized possession
if the right person
once held it
in their hands,
wore it,
or signed it.

For those we admire
but may never meet,
or those we loved
but will never see again
in this life,
we cling to
any connection
we can find,

cherishing even
the smallest point
of overlap
between our lives,
whether joined
by time or space
or something else.

Behind the selfishness
and apathy
often poisoning
our world,
we find a refreshing amount
of sentimentality,
binding us
to one another
whether we know it
or not,
forging bonds
that can never
be broken.

TIGHTLY BOUND

You've seen me bleed,
scream, cry,
run and hide,
you've seen me
shake with anxiety,
burn with embarrassment,
and pulse with anger,
you've seen me
win, lose, laugh, and smile,
get married
and kiss my first child,
you've seen me
content, carefree,
mischievous, and wild;
I don't care
what you wear,
how you vote,
or what you believe,
when you're high,
I float,
when you're cut,
I bleed.

Existence

FIREFLIES

On a hot and humid summer's night
many winged things take flight,
though none but the firefly
gives off light, shining briefly
like a lighthouse lantern,
piercing the darkness
for only a moment, retreating then
into the monochromatic evening sky,
where all other winged things fly.

This is the lot of the firefly,
that though there is peace
in the night's reply
of enveloping darkness
within which and whereby
the small, winged bug
may peacefully fly,
it cannot don twilight forever;
the firefly must shine,
regardless of whether
its will and its nature align,

FLY FOR YOU

it must, until
it has withered
and turned to dust,
give of its light
that all may see,
this is its calling,
its destiny.

THE SUN STILL BURNS

Of what consequence
is it to the sun
what others believe
about its existence?

When civilizations
worshiped it as a god,
did the mammoth star
burn more brightly
to confirm its deity?

When wise men fought
regarding its place
in the universe,
did its fiery surface
contract or expand
a single inch
in response to
a well-reasoned argument?

No.

The fires of the sun

FLY FOR YOU

are not stoked
by an observer's belief
in the flames,
but by the nature
of the sun's
very being.

I AM HERE

I am here,
writing to you now,
and no matter the heights
or depths we traverse,
the summits we cheer
or the valleys we curse,
the joys that we share
or the wounds that we nurse,
I am here,
writing to you now.

WHAT SHALL I DO WITH THE WALL?

What shall I do
with the wall?

The stones
have all fallen
to the ground,
as the mortar
by which each
was once bound
to the other
has wasted away;
should I, in bitter regret,
leave the stones
where they lie,
sacrificing not
a single bead of sweat
to rebuild
what has fallen,
what has failed,
a bitter truth
I cannot forget,

or should I gather the stones
and lather the stones
with new mortar,
binding each to each,
rebuilding the wall
until no proof remains
of the once strong
barrier's breach,
until I lie wearied
and smiling
upon the earth,
having traded places
with the derelict wall,
satisfied that though I am spent,
it is steady, strong, and tall?

A BELL RINGS

A bell rings
on the edge of town,
a poor boy
sits at the base
of its tower,
pulling weakly
on the tolling rope,
wondering
if anyone will hear...

J. ANTON DAVIS

THE GROWTH OF FLOWERS

It is amazing
how flowers
flourish
when each
is allowed
to grow
in its own way.

THE LINE

We sat on the beach,
side by side,
looking back and forth
from one another
to the brilliant sunset,
finding ever more elaborate ways
to describe its beauty,
bound to one another
by the same sense
of awe and ecstasy,
of reverence and rapture...
but, even while washed
in the light of each dying ember
of the sun's daily retreat,
I couldn't help but remember
that we, even as we sat so near
on the beach, were separated
by a fine line in the sand,
one etched so subtly,
not by spade or hand,
that it almost went unnoticed,
like a tiny, harmless no-man's-land,

but, even still, it is that line I fear most,
the one that stole my attention
from the setting sun
in which I longed to be engrossed;
why was it ever drawn,
and how long must we wait
before it is gone, washed clean
by the fierce and unstoppable sea,
erased for all eternity?

PREDICTABLE DISTANCE

It is amazing
how distant
a person can be
when we
do not let them
come close
to us.

INNOCENT BEAUTY

Should a flower
be condemned
for its beauty?

While its delicate petals
may wrest admirers
from the passing butterfly,
could the wandering insect
ever rightly accuse
the flower of vanity?

Experience teaches
that it is often
in the moments
of greatest self-forgetfulness,
not least,
that a person
is most captivating.

I'M ASKING YOU

When you need
to catch your breath,
but your world
won't slow down,
what do you do?

...no, I'm asking you.

FALLING SKIES

If the sky began to fall,
many would not want to know,
for blissful ignorance is bliss,
and terror is a daunting foe.

But others would prefer to see,
with open eyes their coming fate,
to make amends, to hold their friends
and family, to cogitate.

We cannot know what we would choose,
to open or to close our eyes,
until we stand in disbelief,
our world beset by falling skies.

GRIEF

Grief
is a ringing bell
inside the quiet
of the mind;
it is a bright,
tinkling sound
which, though soft,
pierces the silence
in a way that
cannot be ignored.

Though many try
to convince themselves
that the sound
does not exist,
its reverberations,
if unaddressed,
will continue to grow
until the one, so afflicted,
can run no farther
from the truth
of its being.

Once acknowledged,
the maddening notes
cannot be destroyed,
only released,
transformed one by one
into wails and tears
until nothing remains,
leaving a quiet mind
that will no longer
thwart the recovery
of a battered
and weary soul.

DO YOU HEAR ME?

We wander the world asking,
"Do you hear me?"
and cling closest to those
who answer, "Yes."

J. ANTON DAVIS

DESERT FLOWERS

The deserts
of life
can be harsh,
extreme,
and unforgiving
environments,
but even
among the sand,
one finds flowers
of immeasurable beauty,
some which grow
nowhere else.

Change

J. ANTON DAVIS

DO YOU HEAR THE ROOSTER CROWING?

Listen, listen,
everyone,
do you hear
the rooster crowing?

The sun has pierced
the morning sky,
the din of waking birds
is growing.

No heavy eyes
or dragging feet
will change the hour
the clock is showing.

Listen, listen,
everyone,
do you hear
the rooster crowing?

AS WE WAIT FOR FALL

The sun hangs high
while weeds grow tall,
insects swarm
as we wait for fall.

Sweat pours down
and night winds squall,
spiders sew
as we wait for fall.

Low yards flood
while cicadas call,
roaches dart
as we wait for fall.

Soon, summer heat
we'll oft recall,
but curse the thought
as we wait for fall.

AN ADULT'S LAMENT

When I was young,
I laid down
in cool, creek water
while its steady current
slid down my back,
never thinking
I had anything to fear
but the claws of a startled crawfish
emerging from beneath
a flat, edgy rock, excavated
for far more important work
than protecting tiny river creatures —
there were dams to be built
and destroyed, after all, within
tight and uncertain deadlines,
determined exclusively
by the amount of time it took
a distracted, teenage lifeguard
to notice we were missing
from the neighborhood pool —
were I to retrace my steps today,
I wouldn't even reach the creek

FLY FOR YOU

for fear of poison ivy, though
even if I did, the smallest splash
of water into my mouth or eyes
would summon an immediate
internal dialogue consisting solely
of wails and lamentations,
each decrying the unjust nature
of my inevitable and impending doom,
soon to be wrought
by some heretofore dormant
flesh or brain-eating amoeba
found only in shallow creeks
of the North Carolina Piedmont
when the wind blows east
and the sun sinks low
in a pinkish-blue sky...
come to think of it,
what a way to die...

OLD STONES

Old stones
line the walk
to my front door,
keeping my path straight
and free from the grasses
that otherwise surround me,
green blades that hide
many fangs and eyes
and through which the fool
and never the wise
goes wandering.

Upon inspection,
near my front door,
I noticed something
I'd not seen before,
a pile of stones,
a fallen mass,
beneath which grew
a shoot of grass.

I froze,

FLY FOR YOU

noting the breach
of grass onto the path
where no green thing grows;
for the first time I confronted
my future, the moment piercing
like a sword, hardly blunted
by the unknowable time
between then and now,
a feeble shield
that will one day fail
and yield a path,
indistinguishable
from the wild grass,
as each guiding stone
that once led me home
will lie in the dust,
unseen and unknown.

J. ANTON DAVIS

THE LAST LEAF OF AUTUMN

When the last leaf of autumn
falls, a quieter, more peaceful
season takes hold,
begone the fiery fuchsia
and blustery winds,
begin the stillness
and the cold.

Though somber seems
the naked oak
as it sits lonely
on a hill,
in truth it rests,
as all things must,
to weather
winter's icy chill.

There is a freedom
in the lull,
when all the world
is fast asleep,
without the need
for vigilance,

FLY FOR YOU

one's mind
breathes fully,
long and deep.

Without this yearly
time to rest,
we could not
carry on,
so autumn hearts
await the day
the last red leaf
is gone.

Perspective

J. ANTON DAVIS

INSECTS IN LAMPLIGHT

One night before bed
when my son was four,
we looked together
at pictures he'd taken
using his very own digital camera –
it was green with a rubber dinosaur case;
Santa had given it to him –
as we scrolled through
the surprisingly artistic photos,
he stopped abruptly
on an image
of countless insects
swarming in the light
of a lamppost, each one
dazzling white in contrast
with the night sky;
as I thought, *huh, I guess*
this is one of those bad pictures
you'd expect to see
on a toddler's camera,
he said, beaming with wonder

and excitement,
"Look at all the stars
in this one!"

I paused, confused, but smiled
when I realized my mistake;
"Wow, you're right." I said,
"They're beautiful!"

J. ANTON DAVIS

AND SO IT GOES

A pebble dreams
of being a rock,
and a rock a boulder,
and a boulder a bluff,
but a bluff wants only
to crumble to pieces,
to exist as smaller,
simpler stuff.

CURSING THE SUN

When I was an owl
I cursed the sun,
as each ray
of its golden light
signaled the end
of yet another night
of hunting and eating.

When I was a flower
I worshiped the sun,
as only its light
had the power
to strengthen
and nourish
my fragile body.

When I was a cave
I ignored the sun,
as my ancient passageways
were unaffected
by either its rising
or its setting.

J. ANTON DAVIS

In time
I have learned
this truth;
that my opinions
of the sun
describe only myself.

BEAUTIFUL BROKENNESS

Can a shard of glass
do anything but cut?

Does it serve
any purpose
once broken
from its pane?

Though, alone,
it is only fit to harm,
when light
passes through it,
refracting in all directions,
in every color,
the shattered glass
becomes part
of a magnificent union
more brilliant
than the last.

J. ANTON DAVIS

CONNECTION

When the moon
first circled the earth,
it did so because
a strong connection
had formed
between the two.

This connection
was never meant
to signal the rejection
of all other planets
who might have won
the moon, or moons
who might have joined
the earth, but the unique
and beautiful bond
that had formed
between two travelers
who were once alone.

WITH GRACE

With grace
we look upon ourselves
at twenty years of age,
"What fools," we say,
"we were in youth,"
we'd seen nothing,
proved nothing,
and knew not patent lie
from truth.

Now, we won't forgive ourselves,
no, not at *this* proficient age,
we've seen too much
and learned too much
to settle for excuses,
"If not clarity or wisdom,
what else is it
that time produces?"

We lash our backs
in punishment
for every imperfection,

but decades hence
we'll understand
our wise and weathered selves,
in truth,
had yet seen nothing,
yet knew nothing,
and wore the ignorance of youth.

NOBLE OR RECKLESS?

They set sail with purpose
and rescuer's pride,
"Onward, onward!"
the captain cried.

Though ship was war-battered
with holes in its side,
"Onward, onward!"
the captain cried.

While taking on water,
the stranded he spied,
"Onward, onward!"
the captain cried.

Though mission was noble
the sailors all died,
"Reckless, reckless!"
their families cried.

J. ANTON DAVIS

THE GREEN THUMB DELUSION

No, I've never been a green thumb,
I just can't get plants to grow,
once I killed a succulent,
impossible, I know.

Sure, I oft forget to water
and I keep them from the sun,
but 'til the day I fade away
I'll ever beat my drum,
that all my woe with things that grow
stems solely from my thumb.

CURSING TREES

Often in this world
we are like a farmer
who picks an apple
from an apple tree,
hoping for a peach.

We return day after day
to the same tree,
expecting that something
will be different,
but each day
we are left
disappointed.

We curse the apple tree,
failing to see
that it is our expectations,
alone,
that leave us confused
and wanting.

J. ANTON DAVIS

THE ROSE HAS THORNS

The rose has thorns
and the kitten has claws,
a true, though uncomfortable, paradox.

We wonder how treasures
so lovely and sweet
could betray our preconceived beliefs.

Our hands bleed
because we misunderstood,
we expected perfection
from merely the good.

Wisdom

J. ANTON DAVIS

ONE YEAR

One year has passed since last
I felt the rumble of
an earthquake coming.

Vibrations grew, I knew
that soon my house would crumble
to the floor.

As pictures crashed I dashed
toward the staircase leading
down to safety.

But fast I fell as hell
broke loose around me
until all was still.

For months I lay, no ray
of sunlight touched my weak
and battered body.

I know not why, but I
one day began to heal

FLY FOR YOU

and grow in strength.

Eventually, debris
gave way as I climbed
inch by inch to freedom.

My body, pale and frail,
felt light as air when I
broke through the ruins.

I left to find a kind
and gentler soil on which
to build a home.

My home now built won't wilt
when rumblings shake the earth
beneath its beams.

For I have gained through pained
defeats the strength to stand
when all else falls.

LIKE SON LIKE FATHER

Recently,
as my infant son
wailed in my face
and would not be
consoled, I thought,
with mild frustration,
*he doesn't even know
what he wants!*

I paused,
then grinned,
embarrassed that I had,
even in my thoughts,
pretended to be
self-possessed
of my own desires.

In truth,
I often feel
like a traveler
with a broken compass,
following directions

FLY FOR YOU

that change
as quickly
as the wind.

J. ANTON DAVIS

A LINE IN THE SAND

A line in the sand
is a cry for a fight,
it demands each man choose,
requires someone to win
and someone to lose,
whether cooperation
was yet within sight.

A gauntlet thrown down
shows a lust for a brawl,
who can then apologize
once a challenge is made
and foes have locked eyes,
only one can walk home
while the other must crawl.

Must the many take cues
from the fiery few,
cannot level heads,
though opposed, stop
division before it spreads,
settling conflicts

by thoughtful review?

SOMEONE I ONCE KNEW

Even if you'd wanted,
there was nothing you could do,
your great sin was reminding me,
of someone I once knew.

YOU SAID YOU WANTED

You said you wanted
to build a house,
so I gave you boards,
a hammer, and nails;
the boards rotted,
the hammer and nails rusted,
and when I asked you
what happened
you said you wanted
to paint a picture.

I bought you canvas,
paints, and brushes,
and when the paint dried up
and the brushes were lost
and the canvas was torn,
I asked you what happened;
you said you wanted
to climb a mountain...
I didn't know what to say
or what I should do,
was I foolish

from the beginning
to have helped you,
would I be cruel
if I didn't support
this dream, too?

Upon reflection, it seems
I may serve you best
by challenging your dreams,
by helping you test
and refine them,
though it may take time
and we may destroy a dream
or two you thought sublime,
I will help you find the calling
that effortlessly fills your life
to its brim, a treasure
more worthwhile
than every caprice
born of fancy or whim.

A DESPERATE EAR

A desperate ear accepts
the counsel of fools,
forgetting
that a fool's confidence
does not wisdom make.

J. ANTON DAVIS

WHEN A DOG BITES

When a dog bites
your hand,
from then on,
you cannot help
but always wonder,
despite the bridge
and water under,
when next he'll spurn
your reprimand.

MOUNTAINTOP

Ten years ago
I stood upon
a mountaintop;
the air was fresh
and crisp, I could
see clearly for miles
in every direction,
and I wanted
for nothing...
it was perfect.

As things
so often go,
I eventually
left my perch
for the woods
and wilds
of the valley,
searching
for something
called "real life."

After a decade

of wandering
through murky forests,
I find myself
on that same
mountaintop,
pondering
what I have learned
since I left.

Though the view
is not as it was
when I, through youthful eyes,
first observed it, the summit
is now more peaceful,
as its endless visibility
stands in stark contrast
to the perpetual
and impenetrable
darkness
through which I walked
on the canopy-laden
valley floor.

Were I to leave
this mountaintop

a second time,
I might never
find my way back,
and even if I did,
it would be through tears
that I looked out
from its peak,
distraught that I had
twice traded
years of clarity
for obscurity,
and thousands of deep,
refreshing breaths
for the intolerable stench
of stagnant earth.

No,
this time I will stay
on the mountaintop,
leaving only
to fell sturdy trees,
for it is here
I will build
my home.

SELF-CONFIDENCE

It is amazing
the self-confidence
we lack
when we are not
being ourselves.

BROAD SEARCHES

I thought the broadest search was best,
I wandered far and wide to find,
a necklace hung upon my chest,
a place which never came to mind.

J. ANTON DAVIS

INSANITY

I bang my head against a wall,
it does not shake, it does not fall,
forgetting what I tried before,
I bang and bang my head some more.

I SOLD MY GUITAR

I sold my guitar
of fifteen years,

What secrets lie
in each taut string?

You'll have to ask
the guitar yourself,

It never told me
anything.

J. ANTON DAVIS

VOICELESS

I placed my voice
within a box,
then blamed the world
when I could not speak.

I PAID IT TWICE

I touched a hot stove
and paid the price;
I took the moment personally
and so I paid it twice.

BEWARE THE KNOCKING AT YOUR DOOR

Beware the knocking
at your door,
though sweet smells glide
across the floor,
resist this cunning snare,
you know not what prowls
the darkness beyond
or how quickly its teeth
may come to bare.

Beware the knocking
at your door,
though celestial chords
rap softly upon your mind
like gentle waves soothing
a lonely shore,
you must neglect
this siren song,
lest you taste
each poison note
softly seeping, even creeping,

FLY FOR YOU

from the unseen hunter's throat.

Beware the knocking
at your door,
for once you open wide
the wooden shield
protecting you, preserving
who you were before,
you will not easily, if ever,
expel your toxic guest,
usurper, and thief,
and even if someday you do,
until then you will find
so much pain
and little relief.

J. ANTON DAVIS

KNOWLEDGE

"I know the answer,"
the well-worn claim
of those who know little.

"I know an answer,"
the oft-used assertion
of those who know much.

Lament

DISCONTENTMENT

More,
more,
more,
more,
more,
more,
more,
more,
more...

It is exhausting enough
to read,
how much more so
to live?

I will stop typing
when you stop dictating.

More,
more,
more,
more,

FLY FOR YOU

more,
more,
more...

J. ANTON DAVIS

HEARTLESS

I placed my heart
within a box,
then blamed the world
when I could not love.

WE USED TO WALK
THE PATH TOGETHER

We used to walk the path together
whenever I stopped by,
arm in arm, slowly wandering,
spying every hidden thing
that grew or crawled
just beneath the surface
of a casual glance;
time waited and watched
like a doting father,
never continuing its journey
until ours was complete.

It was paradise...

It *was* paradise...

One day I visited,
not knowing
you had hidden something
in the woods,
just off the path, something

that bound you tightly
in fear and shame, something
from which you felt
you would never be free;
I asked, as I always did,
if we might take a stroll together,
but you declined, first timidly,
then with ever-growing intensity
as I pressed you further,
until you left me
standing at the gate,
with words you could never take back
ringing in my ears.

We used to walk the path together
whenever I stopped by,
but now we do not walk
or even speak together,
and I will never know why.

ESSE QUAM VIDERI

"To be
rather than
to seem."

Are these words,
in a modern world,
nothing but
a distant dream?

THIS WORLD

O,
that this world
knew more
of compassion
and empathy,
what a better world
it would be.

In many cases,
it seems that
one will only offer
comforting words
to another
that has proven himself
worthy of such care,
one who has shown
that he suffers more
than the giver
of the handkerchief.

If one suspects
that another,

who has exposed his burdens
like an open wound,
suffers less
than himself,
the listener
will slap away
the hand that grasps
for a steadying shoulder,
leaving the wary man
to "find another fool"
who might lend a hand
to such an "able body."

The stinginess
of this world,
forged by the hammers
of comparison
and envy,
is almost too
much to take;
what is lost
by the offering
of a kind word?

O,

and what
is gained?

IN MY HASTE

I swung my sword
to slash your chest
and struck the blow
I sought,
but in my haste
to lay you waste
my ally I forgot,
she stood beside me
ready to
lay down her life
for me,
and so she did,
though by my sword,
quite unexpectedly,
so now I weep
with shaking hands
pressed firmly to my face,
to hide from me
the memory
of torn and bloody lace.

PROPHETS

Why are prophets despised
for speaking across time,
for opening eyes
to truths, forgotten or unknown,
for exposing lies
with proofs that cut
through skin and bone,
in truth, I understand the mob,
the pitchforks, the hunt,
and the groan
of a mind unprepared
for the wisdom and light
it's been shown,
which recoils as if threatened
by this thing, yet unknown,
and the hands, that by the mind
do all that they do,
seize, kill, and bury
the poor soul who argued contrary
to all that they knew.

THE BURIED LEAD

When I feel down
I seek to find
just what it is that ails me,
as you are always
standing there,
it must be you that fails me.

In many years
I'll see the truth
and fall into despair,
I missed the simple,
buried lead
that you were always there.

J. ANTON DAVIS

A THOUSAND PEARLED OYSTERS

Treasure
seems almost
drawn to you,
powerless to resist
even the smallest effort
on your part
to seek
and to find it;
gold clings to your pick
at the first swing
and prize fish
fight for your hook
when you cast a line.

How tragic, then,
that though treasures spring
from all you touch, in vain
you feast on gold
and wear your catch
like jewelry,
wondering why you're starving
and smell like the tide;

FLY FOR YOU

you sit among
a thousand pearled oysters,
with no clue
how to get inside.

OVERKILL

I walked the forest on my land
and found a tree that could not stand,
to fell the slouching tree I'd found
I burned the forest to the ground.

HUMAN NATURE

What is it
about human nature
that drives us
to behold beauty
and not simply
appreciate it,
but desire to take it
for ourselves?

If each person
plucked a star
from the sky,
the magnificence
of the cosmos
would be lost.

If every visitor
to the Eiffel Tower
left with wrought iron
in their pocket,
the Pride of Paris
would be dismantled

in days.

In our lust
to take beauty
for ourselves,
we cannot help
but destroy
that which we find
beautiful.

We must learn
to appreciate
without having,
to admire
without coveting,
and to love
without desiring,
for what loveliness,
save One,
can survive
our insatiable
cravings?

OF PUPPIES AND RABBITS

The rabbit flees all things,
avoiding enemies
and friends, alike.

The puppy approaches all things,
meeting pleasures
and threats
with the same vigor.

Neither is wrong,
but how much better
if each had the mind of man,
allowing both to assess
a situation before acting?

The rabbit
would not forfeit the help
of small children
offering vegetables,
and the puppy
would not invite the claws
of wary house cats.

J. ANTON DAVIS

How unfortunate, then,
that man, who has this mind,
often ignores it,
preferring instead the blunt,
reactionary life
of puppies and rabbits...

Consider

SEAWORTHY SHIPS

Were I to build
a ship for the sea,
where might I
test its limits
and cut its teeth?

Should I wade it
into placid waters,
flanked by beaches,
protected from waves?

Should I loose the sails
upon a lake,
observing
how the wind behaves?

Or should I find
a stormy night,
and see how long
the vessel braves?

We must sharpen

FLY FOR YOU

each belief we hold
by grinding it
against its opposite,
lest we should taste
a stormy sea
as wreckage floats
on top of it.

J. ANTON DAVIS

PUDDLE JUMPING

We are often like children
stomping in a puddle,
startled by the water
splashing in our eyes
and angry
with whoever
is causing it,
never considering
the answer may lie
at our feet
in the water's reflection.

THE LAST TO DRINK

As we water
our plants
each day,
moving slowly
from bed to bed
and pot to pot,
we learn
it is the flower
that drinks last
which wilts.

Once we have poured
our draught
upon the first rows,
thoughtlessly giving
as if our supply
were endless,
we catch our mistake
and learn to ration
what remains
as each plant
receives less

and less.

The glut
of the first
is the want
of the last.

We must remember
when we water,
if the same flower
is always
the last to drink,
we will soon
need to tend it
no more...

TUG OF WAR

Life is a constant
tug of war,
and there are
many worthy ropes
to pull.

Who has the strength
to grasp them all,
who has the fire
and the fuel?

And if that
boundless brawn
were found
within one person,
do recall,
two hands alone
we each possess,
to grab new ropes
old ropes must fall.

WHEN GLASS BREAKS

When glass breaks,
must we all rush
to clean it up?
Are not some needed
to discover the cause
of its breaking?
Are not others called
to make clear the area
to protect those passing by?
Still more must decide
how to avoid similar,
future destruction.
What do we gain
by demanding
that the cleaner make plans,
the planner ensure safety,
the protector investigate,
and the investigator sweep?

Must we all respond the same
to prove we care
that a glass has broken?

THE DEATH OF "ME"

Were I to choose
a ten-foot ladder
to scale
a fifty-foot wall,
I would never reach
the top.

Though I might curse
the ladder
for its inadequacy,
is the misunderstanding
the ladder's
or my own?

I have asked it
to do what it cannot,
as it was not built
to reach such heights.

In the same way,
we must not ask
of people

what they cannot
give us; mainly
purpose,
meaning,
or value.

When we do so,
we heap burdens
on their shoulders
that cannot be borne,
weights which will either
crush the carrier
or be tossed aside
in the interest
of self-preservation,
as they have no choice
beyond the death of "me"
or the death of "us."

Take Heart

A RAY OF SUNLIGHT

Dark clouds fill the sky
while cold air crashes
against upturned collars,
a light drizzle falls
upon lonely streets.

A bowed head rises
to meet the gray
and lonely world,
a tired sigh
of wandering smoke
lingers in the empty air.

A passing cloud parts
for only a moment,
a ray of sunlight pierces
the neglected sky,
a heavy heart lifts
in grateful reply.

REJECTION

When I'm fearful of rejection,
I find it everywhere,
no matter where I run or hide,
rejection's always there.

But when I drop my shield,
and sheathe my ready blade,
I learn rejection's bluster,
is a feeble masquerade.

If it's really even there,
its wounds are often slight,
I find rejection's bark,
to be much meaner than its bite.

SIMPLE CERTAINTIES

While troubled hearts ache
and needless wounds bleed,
the waves unceasingly crash and recede.

While masses trade shackles
for shiny new chains,
the moon unflinchingly waxes and wanes.

While struggling souls add
to untenable debts,
the sun repeatedly rises and sets.

While fevers run hot
and medicines fight,
the birds greet the morn
and the crickets the night.

FINDING FREEDOM

I thought
that freedom lie
on the edge of the world,
beyond the distractions
and expectations
of everyday life,
and indeed it does,
but not there alone.

I have found freedom
even in my home,
where my responsibilities
are greatest
and where I cannot hide
behind affected expressions
of tranquility and sublimity;
I have learned
that freedom springs forth
not from the soil
of uncharted lands,
but from the fertile loam
of curiosity,

self-expression,
and simplicity.

Freedom,
in its deepest sense,
is mine,
and I will take it
with me
wherever I go.

FACING LIONS

Often in life,
it is the dreams
we care about most
that make us tremble
when they come
within reach.

We stand
before these dreams,
staring blankly,
as if facing down
a lion,
its teeth bared
beneath fiery eyes,
our uncertainty
magnified
by the fearless
demeanor
of our adversary.

If, however,
we can muster

the courage
to take one step
forward,
the lion's fangs
will dull slightly,
sending a twinge
of adrenaline and power
through our tense muscles,
the first suggestions
of a thrilling chase,
one where we
are the hunter
and the lion
the prey.

While the lion
will roar
at this brazen challenge
of its strength,
if we can take
another step
forward,
the first signs of fear
will flash across
the monster's face,

as one paw,
ever so slightly,
slides backward.

Our next decision
will be the most important
and will determine
the outcome
of this delicate encounter;
it is then,
for the first time,
that we will feel
the blazing heat
of the lion's breath
and the thunder
of its roar,
and it is then
that we must decide.

We must decide
whether our first steps
were a foolish,
dangerous bluff,
projecting more courage
than we possessed,

or a sign of our strength,
a subjugation of our fears,
and an acceptance
of the fight to come.

What, then,
will we do?

You and I both
will discover
the answer
when we are,
with all hope,
face to face
with the teeth,
claws, and roar
of an elusive dream,
one that is too proud
to be captured
or tamed
without a fight.

Consider the risks
of picking
such a fight;

FLY FOR YOU

consider also
the risks
of not doing so...

A LIGHT AMONG DEATH

There is a light
among death
that shines brighter
than any darkness
which mourning brings.

Lives remembered,
journeys celebrated,
souls liberated
from an imperfect world,
rising to new heights
of peace, joy,
and understanding.

The souls
of those left behind
are branded
with the marks
of their loved ones,
marks that will become
badges of pride
once their wounds

FLY FOR YOU

have sealed shut,
finally protected
from the unforgiving,
fiery storms of recollection.

One day,
all that will remain
is joy, born from
deep bonds
of friendship and love,
forged smile by smile
and kiss by kiss;
until that day comes,
we cheer and cry,
laugh and weep,
remembering those
who were first
to sleep.

J. ANTON DAVIS

AUDACIOUS LIFE

What brazen mockery of death,
that such an innocent is born,
surrounded by the rot of war,
upon a dark apartment floor,
which only candle flames adorn.

No doctor can to her attend,
this mother in the throes of birth,
her family and her neighbors strive,
to keep the babe and mom alive,
to loose new life upon the earth.

The baby first to them appeared,
a lifeless child, pale and blue,
but 'lisa would not be denied,
her precious life, and so she cried,
and turned a more vivacious hue.

Amid the bombs and rifle fire,
there springs life to contradict,
destruction and the pain of loss,
each a mighty albatross,

which war cannot but help inflict.

J. ANTON DAVIS

THE BEACH REEDS SWAY

As the light breeze
of each morning comes,
rolling sand across
lonely dunes,
beach reeds sway
in wandering winds,
gently, then forcefully,
then still again.

Waves crash softly
on the shore,
driven by
a waxing tide,
minnows dance
in shallow surf,
sea foam tumbles,
seagulls glide.

Rays of sunlight
bathe the sand
still chilly
from the night before,

FLY FOR YOU

waking crabs
creep cautiously
gnats take flight,
fiddlers bore.

Though I sit
in leather shoes,
behind a desk,
far away,
I find great peace
in distant shores
where seagulls call
and beach reeds sway.

UNSEEN EFFORTS

I walked one step
and no one cared,
then at one hundred
one man stared,

five hundred earned
a clap or two,
one thousand felt
like déjà vu,

three thousand won
a meager crowd,
five thousand made
some cheer aloud,

eight thousand brought
the local news,
ten thousand spurred
some interviews,

one hundred thousand
steps I strode,

FLY FOR YOU

before the fame
and fortune flowed,

still millions cried,
"He must be new!"
But I knew
that it wasn't true...

Me

J. ANTON DAVIS

"OTHER"

You jumped and cheered,
screamed and cried,
when you asked if I
felt the same, I said yes.
I lied.

You danced and sang,
gathered here, then there,
we high-fived, I smiled.
I was miserable.
You weren't aware.

You laughed and hugged,
invited and accepted,
though in the end
we were both performing,
unknowingly, the part
we thought the other expected.

What an odd, lonely season,
what uncomfortable skin,
I could walk on the moon

FLY FOR YOU

or hike across Mars
and feel less "other"
than I did back then.

J. ANTON DAVIS

I AM WHO I AM

I am who I am,
I'm not who I'm not,
begone my passion and ambition,
along with every apparition,
each that never to fruition
came, when counter to my lot.

PEACEMAKER

I hold no banner
or flag,
is that okay?

Will you hear
and love me
anyway?

J. ANTON DAVIS

YOU LIKED MY SMILE

You said you liked my smile,
I grinned from ear to ear for days,
but that cheap high only lasted a little while,
after that, I couldn't let you see me
without it, I couldn't take the look
on your face when you saw it was gone,
so I went on smiling,
even when I bled, even when I cried,
I smiled even when I felt dead inside,
years of lies and self-denial,
all because you liked my smile.

WIND-UP DOLL

I spent so much
of my life
as a wind-up doll,
banging cymbals together
at breakneck speed
with no ability to stop
or slow down;
didn't you see
the panic in my eyes
and the shallow breaths
I took whenever we spoke?
If you did, you didn't show
even an ounce of understanding
or compassion, a fact
which made me bitter for years
anytime I remembered
our conversations.

Now, comforted and protected,
humbled and sharpened,
by the impenetrable shield
and merciless sword

that are, both together, time,
I understand your inaction
and apparent apathy;
you were never cruel
or callous,
just lost, uncertain
like me.

LIKE ME

I just wanted you
to like me.

I knew nothing
about myself
and took no real shape
in the world,
flowing like water
to any space
that would hold me,
guided by nothing
but proximity
and availability,
searching for a place
to settle,
to be at rest,
to be at peace.

I wanted something
you could never give,
but even so,
did I really deserve

to feel so foolish,
as if, by seeking your approval,
I was embarrassing myself
in some unforgivable way?

In the end,
I guess you were right...
what was I thinking?

I'M NO FUN

"When I'm at my best,
I'm fun.
When I'm at my worst,
I'm not."
...said everyone, ever.

Don't worry
about being fun
all the time.

J. ANTON DAVIS

WANDERER

I was made to wander
down untrod paths,
taught to search
for something new
on each trip
into the woods,
never knowing
what that something was,
but never doubting
its existence.

Remembering

J. ANTON DAVIS

TREEHOUSE

What a dream it now is
to picture me there,
my back in warm grass,
eyes to the sky,
crafting a treehouse
with my mind's eye.

The fifty-foot oaks
stood side-by-side,
strong, steady, eternal,
leaves swaying in the summer breeze,
my head in the clouds,
my heart in the trees.

There was nothing grander
than what I could see,
bridges here, turrets there,
a boundless earth beneath my feet,
my paradise in boughs,
my blissful retreat.

While many years have passed

FLY FOR YOU

with canopies still bare,
those mighty oaks bring peace
and stir no feelings of regret,
for I now have a daydream
that I never will forget.

FREE

Chlorine in the air,
in my hair,
bright lights dancing
on the water
while we ran, laughed,
and sang, never wondering
what we looked like
or if something we said
was stupid or embarrassing;
we were young, wild,
joyful, and free,
as free as any person
can be.

ME. I DO.

I didn't think I would mind
that they changed it;
who cares for which game
the lines and nets
are painted and hung?
I like pickleball more
than tennis, anyway...

But, that's not how it looked
when we played
on Thanksgiving,
father and sons
surrounded by lofty pines
and sunshine,
good company
and laughter.

That's not how it looked
when I asked you
the deepest questions
I could muster
in the unmoored

and wandering
moments of my youth,
hoping a father's words
could heal my pain
and bring clarity
to my scattered mind.

That's not how it looked
when we threw down our bikes,
rushing onto the court
as our shorts
still dripped with pool water,
pretending to be serious
tennis players
while continually stopping
to laugh
the instant a joke
hit just the right chord
of absurd, boyhood humor.

That's not how it looked
in the countless memories
held in my mind,
aching now, reminding me
that all things must change,

even those that represent
the very best of our lives...

But who cares
about an old tennis court,
anyway?

Me.
I do.

J. ANTON DAVIS

SUMMER DAYS

A warm summer day
is a salve to the soul,
it eases one's mind
and makes one whole.

The sun on one's skin
is a blanket of calm,
a loving embrace,
a restorative balm.

A SOFTER KISS

Has there ever been
a softer kiss,
with confidence
I tell you this,
there hasn't been
a single one,
that kissed me softer
than the sun.

J. ANTON DAVIS

AVOIDING SLEEP

I still cannot sleep,
so why not write?
I'll try to make magic
by the end of the night,

If I lie long enough
on my carpeted floor,
it follows that brilliance
will come to the fore,

Eyes closed with my hands
just resting on keys,
hoping ideas will but
come on a breeze,

No luck for tonight,
as surely you see,
I'm writing of writing,
it's bedtime for me.

ACKNOWLEDGEMENTS

Thank you to my wife, Alexandra, who has always encouraged me in my writing and who humors me even when I ask if I can read her a new poem just as her eyes are closing for the night.

Thank you to my boys, James and Liam, for being the fun-loving, thoughtful, and wonderful (very) young men they have already grown up to be. Thank you also to my boys for inspiring the poem, *Fly for you*, that gives this book its name.

Thank you to my dad, John, who taught me at a young age to dream and that someone can be both an artist and a working professional.

Thank you to my mom, Kathy, who reads everything I write and who has always sung my praises from the rooftops, even when I didn't think I deserved it.

Thank you to my brothers, sisters, and

friends, as well as their families, who have always supported me and who bring me so much joy and happiness.

Lastly, thank you to all of my readers! You both know who you are...(where is my winking emoji when I need it!) In all honesty, thank you to everyone who has ever read my poetry. I appreciate you connecting with my words and thoughts, whether you think in the end that my writing is high art or not worth the paper it's printed on. In the end, it is neat to join you all in conversations across space and time, wrestling through the great joys, sorrows, and mysteries of life.

AUTHOR BIOGRAPHY

J. Anton Davis is a husband, father, attorney, and poet. A born-and-raised North Carolinian, he lives in Raleigh with his wife, Alexandra, and sons, James and Liam.

Though Davis has written poetry and fiction privately for over 20 years, in 2019 he launched his website, JAntonPoetry.com, to begin sharing his writing publicly. His poems focus on the deep meaning hidden within the seemingly insignificant and mundane.

Beyond writing poetry and fiction, Davis enjoys exploring local Greenway trails, playing soccer and pickleball, and spending time with his family and friends.

J. Anton and Alexandra Davis
Summer 2024

FOLLOW THE AUTHOR

Keep up with the writings of J. Anton Davis by following one or more of the following steps:

- Visit his website, JAntonPoetry.com.
- Sign up for the J. Anton Poetry Substack.
- Follow @jantonpoetry on Instagram.
- Like the J. Anton Poetry Facebook page.
- Follow @jantonpoetry on X.
- Follow him on Goodreads.
- Email him at JAntonPoetry@gmail.com to let him know what you thought of *Fly for you*.

If you enjoyed this book, remember to leave a review on Amazon.com and Goodreads.com. Also, don't forget to tell your friends, family, and social media connections about *Fly for you* and let your local bookstores know that you would like to see works by J. Anton Davis on their shelves.

Thank you for reading!

ISBN: 978-1-7355407-7-1 (Paperback)
ISBN: 978-1-7355407-8-8 (eBook)

OTHER WORKS

Love is: A former magistrate's poetic reflections on love and marriage in a county courthouse
ISBN: 978-1-7355407-0-2 (Paperback)
ISBN: 978-1-7355407-1-9 (eBook)
ASIN: B0968VW1ZS (Audiobook)

Oak City Tales
ISBN: 978-1-7355407-2-6 (Paperback)
ISBN: 978-1-7355407-3-3 (eBook)

YOUR OWN POETRY

YOUR OWN POETRY

YOUR OWN POETRY

YOUR OWN POETRY

YOUR OWN POETRY

www.ingramcontent.com/pod-product-compliance
Lightning Source LLC
Chambersburg PA
CBHW052136070526
44585CB00017B/1855